Take a Seat!

Contents

Pull Up a Chair

Chairs and other seats come in many shapes and sizes, but they are all designed for sitting on. Some seats are high, some seats are low. Some have arms and some do not.

How many different kinds of seats can you find in this picture?

3

Made to Be Carried

Long ago, special chairs were used to carry some people. In those days, the roads were very dirty, and ladies wore long gowns. Instead of walking, rich ladies would "take a chair."

Sedan chair

4

In some places, important people are still carried in chairs.

5

A Royal Seat

On special occasions, some important people such as kings and queens sit on a special chair called a *throne*. Many thrones are very old and very beautiful. However, they are not usually comfortable to sit on.

6

This throne from Egypt is more than 3,000 years old.

This throne from Turkey is made with gold and precious stones.

7

Chairs of the Past

Many years ago, only rich people had chairs. But over the years, more and more people could afford to buy them. Many people worked as chair-makers and chair-menders.

This chair-mender is collecting broken chairs.

8

Why do you think this chair is called a ladder chair?

These old chairs were all made by hand. This made them expensive pieces of furniture.

9

Making an Armchair

Many people like sitting in a comfortable armchair. Look how an armchair is made.

1 Build the frame.

2 Cover the frame with foam.

3 Cut and sew cloth to cover the chair and to make cushions.

4 Cover the chair with cloth.

5 Stuff the cushions with foam.

Take a seat!

11

Just for Kids

Around 300 years ago, people started making special chairs for children. Today, most small children have their own special chairs. There are chairs for eating in, chairs for swinging in, and chairs that have matching tables.

Do you know the story of Goldilocks and the Three Bears? Whose chair was just right?

12

13

Work Seats

Many chairs are designed to help people do their jobs. Hairdressers have chairs that go up and down. Dentists have chairs that tip people back. People who work at desks have special chairs, too.

Today, there are even giant balls to sit on. Some students and office workers use them to help prevent backache!

14

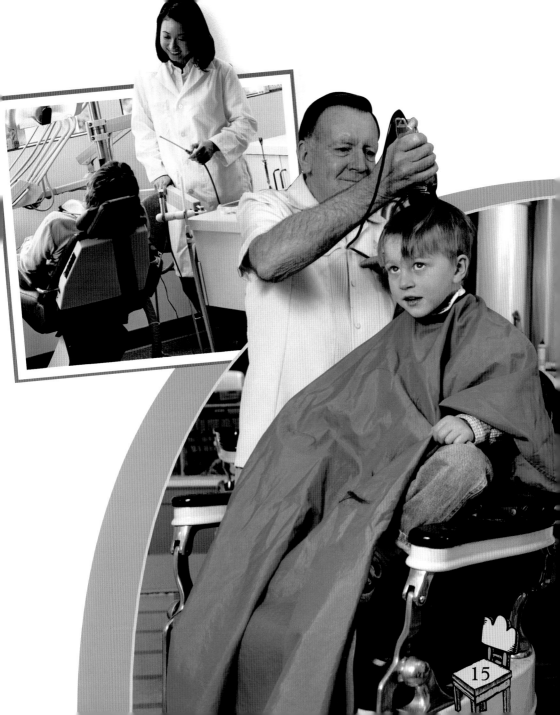

Seats for Going Places

People need seats when they travel. There are seats for road trips and seats for air trips. Many of these seats have special features that help keep people safe.

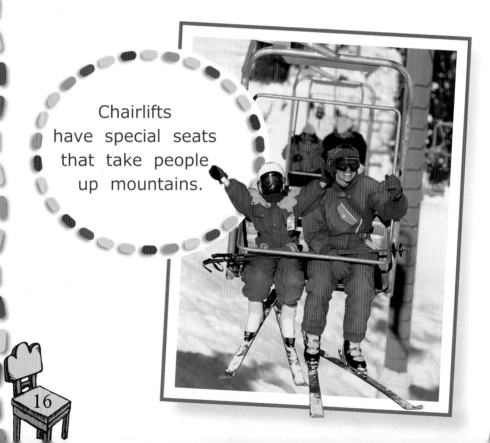

Chairlifts have special seats that take people up mountains.

16

Seats for Fun

Many rides at amusement parks have special seats. They spin, bounce, or even fly. These seats have safety belts or bars that stop people from falling out.

Which ride would you like to try?

Chairs That Help

Wheelchairs help many people. There are wheelchairs for everyday use, wheelchairs for sports-people, and even wheelchairs that can climb stairs.

The first wheelchairs were made of wood. They were very heavy.

Wild and Wacky Chairs

People have created some very unusual chairs. What do you think chairs of the future will look like?

This fruit chair is a work of art. Do you think it would be comfortable to sit on?

23

Index

Lost!

Written by Christine Keighery ◆ Illustrated by Julia Crouth